COMPUTERS AND YOU

Computers are becoming a more and more important part of everyday life for most people in Western countries. They will change our lives in important ways. Some of these changes will help us to lead more interesting and rewarding lives. Others are a threat to our environment, to world peace and to the health of our minds and bodies.

Computers and You examines the effect that computers will have on our lives. It describes some of their advantages and some of their disadvantages, and asks how *you* will deal with the effects of the computer age.

Ian Litterick is an expert on microcomputer systems, a writer and an inventor. Chris Smithers has long experience of illustrating computers. Both author and designer share an interest in helping non-experts to understand, and so to control, computer technology.

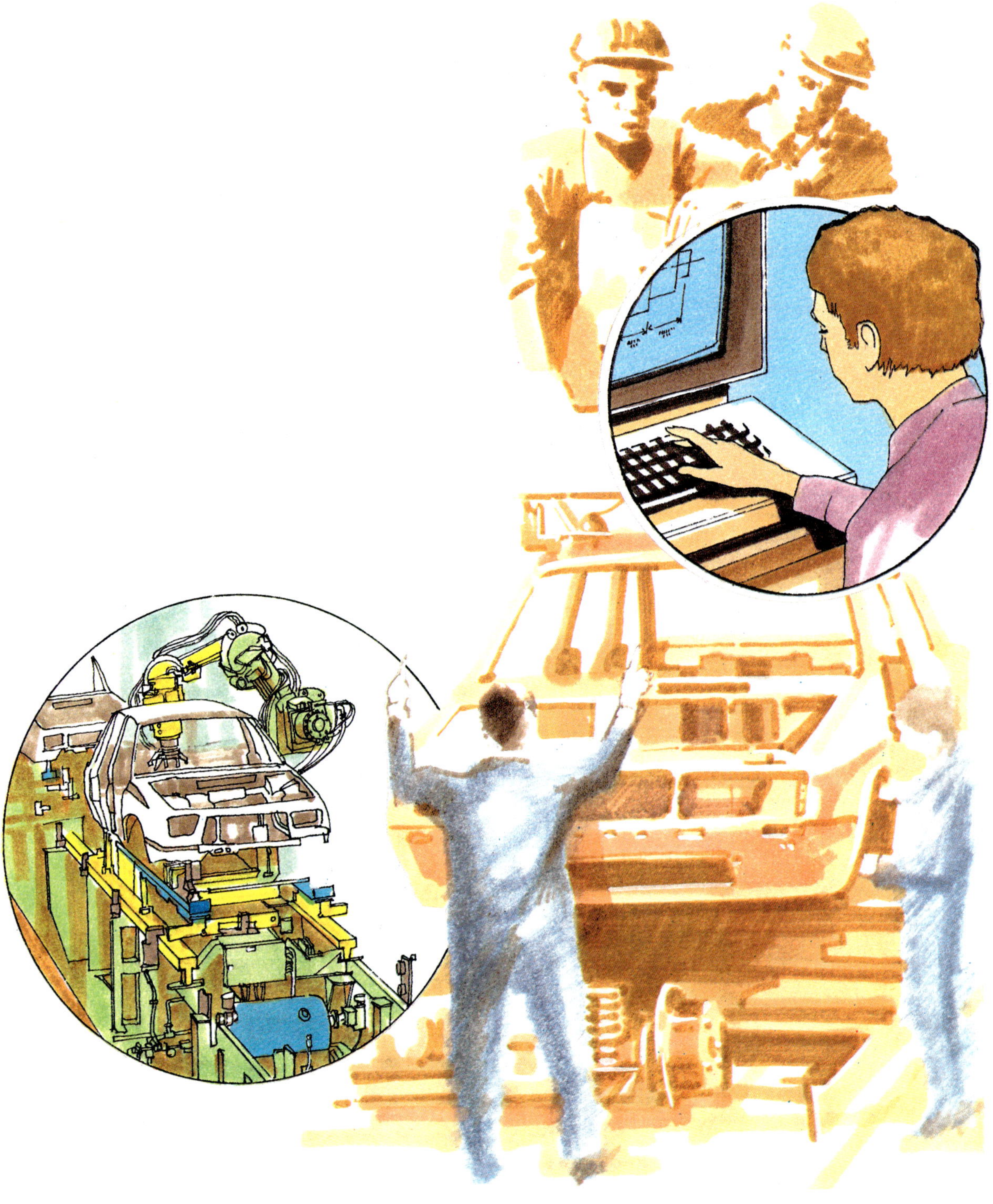

The Age of Computers
COMPUTERS AND YOU

Ian Litterick
Designed by Chris Smithers

Wayland

Other books in this series
Computers in Everyday Life
How Computers Work
The Story of Computers
Robots and Intelligent Machines
Programming Computers

ISBN 0 85078 260 0

© Copyright 1983 Wayland Publishers Limited
First published in 1983 by
Wayland Publishers Limited
49 Lansdowne Place, Hove,
East Sussex BN3 1HF, England

Typeset in the U.K. by Wordsmiths, Street
Printed in Italy by G. Canale and C.S.p.A., Turin
Bound in the U.K. at The Pitman Press, Bath

Contents

Computopia *6*
Computyrannia *8*
Progress and disruption *10*
Computers and the environment *12*
Work or unemployment? *16*
Working life *20*
Working with computers *24*
Education and training *28*
Big Brother *30*
Computers and the developing world *34*
War and peace *38*
Will computers need us? *41*

Glossary *44*
Finding out more *46*
Index *47*

Computopia

We know that computers are changing our world day by day. But it is much harder to tell whether the change is for the better or for the worse. There are two sides to the story. 'Computopia' is one of them.

Below *In Computopia, many people work at home, travel less, and spend more time with their families.*

Computopia is an imaginary place where all the advantages of a highly computerized society are to be found. Human knowledge and skills – in science, art and recreation – develop faster than ever before. Information on any subject can be reached in seconds.

People do not have to work much. Working hours are short, holidays are long. People spend many years of their lives learning – often going back to college two or three times as adults. Few workers have to do unpleasant, boring or dangerous jobs, as they are now practically all done by robots and computers. Many people work without having to leave their homes.

Working people know that their work is valuable, as it cannot easily be done by a machine – their human skills are called for.

People do not travel much: they can communicate with anybody they like at the touch of a few buttons. They can see people, talk to them, or just exchange written messages, all in an instant.

Everybody is looked after. The elderly can get in touch with other people whenever they want to, and their needs are catered for. The disabled can lead near-normal lives thanks to their computer-aided artificial limbs. The

Above *Care for the elderly, protection of the environment, little crime and an efficient public transport system are all features of Computopia.*

blind can 'see' with the help of computerized scanners, and can read and write thanks to computers which talk to them and understand their speech.

Many diseases have been wiped out: by checking computerized medical records, it is usually possible to find the causes of a new disease and to eradicate it before too many people have suffered from it.

Crime has practically disappeared. Property is protected by networks of burglar alarms. Criminals can easily be traced thanks to the information collected by computer systems all over the country – indeed, all over the world.

People live this pleasant life in the knowledge that thanks, in part, to computers, they are not harming the world's ecology: they are not wasting the world's limited stocks of energy like oil and coal, because their central heating systems are computer-controlled; and they are not polluting their atmosphere with poisonous gases or their rivers with poisonous liquids.

Nor are they living at the expense of people in poorer countries, who are also enjoying the advantages which cheap computer systems bring.

Computyrannia

The other side of the story from 'Computopia' is 'Computyrannia', where the use of the computer tyrannizes its citizens and causes much misery and little benefit.

Below *In Computyrannia, many people are unemployed. Those who do have work find their jobs as machine minders boring, and many of them suffer from such occupational ailments as eyestrain and backache.*

In Computyrannia many of the people are unemployed. They feel that they are wasting their lives as they draw money from the state and contribute nothing.

If they are lucky enough to find work, then it is likely to be as a mere machine minder: keeping an eye on a battery of computer-controlled machines in case a warning light comes on, or feeding information into a word processing system. All of it is mindless and boring, a working life dominated by the demands of machines.

If they work with computers they risk getting occupational complaints – backache, eyestrain, cataracts and other illnesses.

The high level of unemployment has resulted in social unrest and a sharp increase in the amount of crime. Political terrorists take advantage of the discontent and bombings and kidnappings are daily news.

But the state manages to keep its position thanks to its intelligence services, which quickly identify the terrorists through communications between computers. Many people who

Above *Pollution, violence, and repressive police methods are commonplace in Computyrannia.*

have voiced dissident views, often long ago, have been arrested. Others are arrested or mysteriously lose their jobs for no apparent reason. Their friends assume they must be on some computer blacklist, and worry that they, too, may suffer.

Fraud and tax fiddles are almost unheard of. It is practically impossible to buy anything with cash – nobody will accept it because it is too easily stolen. Credit cards are essential for many purchases, but an unpaid account in the past can make it impossible to get one. It is known that all credit and bank accounts are regularly checked by the tax authorities.

Because so few people now travel to work, the public transport systems have become worse and worse. Although taxes are high, the roads are badly kept and congested, as most of the money goes to paying the unemployed.

And it is widely known that in the developing countries where the computers are made, working conditions are poor and their societies are being completely disrupted by the new work.

Progress and disruption

Progress and disruption often go hand in hand. Change brings problems as well as benefits. The new technology of the computer age is bringing very radical changes. It has rightly been called the computer revolution.

Computopia and Computyrannia are not necessarily different places, but may be different ways of looking at the same computerized society. They show how the same developments may have different results depending on how governments and people react to them.

The Industrial Revolution, which started in about 1760, happened over a period of a hundred years. It caused disruption and misery for those whose lives were torn apart by the changes. Some of the people who lost their jobs as a result of the changes, made new lives in better conditions. But others were less lucky.

We have the advantage over our eighteenth- and nineteenth-century ancestors in that we know the sort of results that the Industrial Revolution produced, and can predict some, at least, of the results of the microelectronic revolution.

The machines themselves are unbiased. They can be used to make life easier, to expand our human capabilities. Or they can be used to control us, to harm people and our environment.

It is rare that a change which benefits some people does not harm someone else. How do we ensure that these

Above *The Industrial Revolution did not improve the lives of everyone who left the farms and found work in factories and mines.*

changes bring the 'greatest good to the greatest number'? Or will they merely benefit a minority at the expense of many other people? These are our dilemmas:

Work How will we share it with machines and with each other?

Leisure How will we use our new leisure, and who will pay for it?

Education and training How will we pay for it, and what will we learn?

Ecology How will we use computers to protect and not ruin the world in which we live?

Privacy How will we use the vast amounts of information which computers will hold about us, without invading each other's privacy?

Development What will the effect be on the poorer countries of the world?

War and peace How can the new technology be used to support the idea of peace rather than to encourage war and destruction?

Top to bottom *Society must now decide how best to use computers – in education, leisure, the preservation of peace, and work.*

Computers and the environment

Compared with many other modern developments – the motor vehicle, air travel, fertilizers and nuclear power, for example – microcomputers do very little harm to the world in which we live.

Above and below *Sand and petroleum are turned into the silicon and plastic used to make a computer.*

The main material that microcomputer chips are made out of is silicon, and silicon is just purified sand. Indeed, silicon is one of the commonest elements in the world. There is no possibility that we could ever use up all the sand in the world by building too many computers!

But silicon is one of the least significant of the materials that go into a computer. The outside of the computer is generally made of plastic or steel. Plastic is made from petroleum and requires energy to make. Steel is a metal based on iron, and the steel-making process requires vast amounts

Above *It requires a lot of energy to turn iron into steel.*
Right *The first computers used hundreds of vacuum tubes like this one.*

of energy for heat.

The computer uses glass (also energy-intensive to make) for a screen and a number of other rarer materials – including gold – for some of the wiring and switch contacts.

But it is also true to say that computers themselves are getting smaller and more compact. As they do so they use smaller amounts of these materials. While we should always keep an eye on the use of the world's resources, it is unlikely that computers are going to cause many shortages.

They are also, now, very economical to run. The first computers used vacuum tubes (valves) instead of transistors to work. These tubes needed a lot of electricity – as much as a small power station would produce. And because the tubes gave out so much heat, the first computers needed more energy for air conditioning to cool them down!

A modern microcomputer uses no more electricity than a small light bulb, and needs no air conditioning. Even the manufacturing process does not use much power compared with, say, making a motor vehicle.

At the moment computers use a lot of

Above *The widespread use of screens to display information means that fewer trees will have to be destroyed to make paper.*

paper. Much computer work is still printed out on to paper, often as continuous folded 'listing' paper. Many trees are pulped to make this paper, which is often completely wasted – it may be thrown away without even being looked at, for much computer output is so detailed that nobody can face trying to understand it! But many more trees are cut down to make newspapers, or to turn forest into farmland.

The more trees that are destroyed, the fewer there are to convert the air's carbon dioxide back into oxygen – the gas which we need to breathe in order to live. Tree felling on a large scale also causes soil erosion and climatic changes, increasing the risk of the world becoming a desert.

Fortunately, as computers and networks become more common there will be less need to print things out on paper because we will be able to read them on our screens. But the so-called 'paperless office' where everything is done on screens and never on paper, is almost certainly wishful thinking. Paper is too convenient to be completely discarded in favour of the screen.

The harm that computers can do to the environment is far outweighed by the benefits that they can bring. Microprocessors can control heating systems so that less fuel is used. Computer programs can be used to show us what will happen if we dam a river, increase the number of fish we catch, or cut down a forest.

Computers enable us to create better designs for such things as bridges, electric motors, motor cars and aircraft – so that less raw materials are used in

Left and below *Computers will help designers, farmers, and many other people, to make better use of the time, money, and materials available to them.*

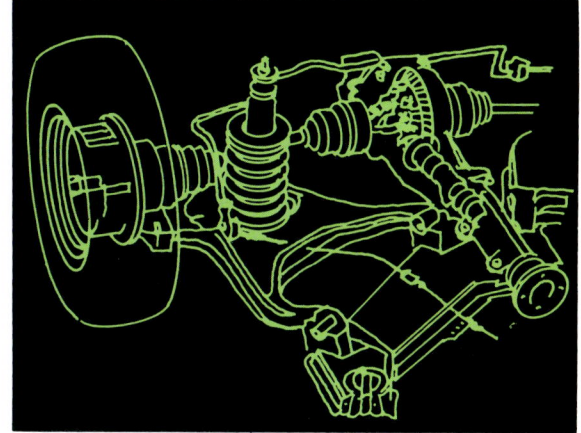

the building or use of them.

They have been used to stop the wastage of food in hospitals by calculating exactly what meals are needed for each patient. Farmers use them to calculate the right mix of animal feeds and of fertilizer, to avoid waste.

Weather forecasters rely heavily on computers, which are already helping to make forecasting more accurate. Farmers are only one of many groups which benefit from accurate forecasts, allowing them to calculate the best moment for sowing and harvesting. A single forecast can stop a whole crop being ruined by a storm or a frost.

Preventing waste is one of the most useful things that computers can do. They could surely help us to avoid destroying our planet and its life forms.

Work or unemployment?

Of all the aspects of life that the computer revolution is going to change, it must be our working lives which are going to be affected most. But is it going to be a change for the better?

The biggest question is: will there be enough work left to go round after the computer revolution? In the late 1970s, some 'prophets of doom' predicted that one in seven people would be unemployed by the late 1980s. At that time, one in twenty-five were unemployed, and this was regarded as an unacceptably high level of unemployment.

With one in seven people already unemployed in the early 1980s, and unemployment still rising, many experts still thought that it was merely 'cyclical'. That is to say, they thought that it was just the result of a temporary recession, and would go away again when the recession was over.

Below *The loss of factory jobs caused by computers may result in some people returning to traditional handicraft industries.*

Right *Word processors and robots have already replaced some of the boring or unpleasant jobs in offices and factories.*

But would it go away again? What chance has a school leaver of finding a job? What chance has the fifty-year-old who has just been made redundant of ever finding a job again?

'There is no doubt that some jobs are disappearing thanks to computers. Some typists' jobs, for example, are being replaced by word-processors, while factory workers' jobs are fast disappearing as robots take over assembly line duties. Robots take over the dangerous, boring and unpleasant jobs, as well as some of the easier ones.

Repair jobs are disappearing in the telephone industry as new, computer-based electronic exchanges replace older, unreliable mechanical ones.

The Industrial Revolution also caused a lot of unemployment as handicraft jobs like weaving were taken over by machines. But after a few decades, everything sorted itself out and new jobs were created in new industries, so giving new work to those who had been displaced.

Some people argue that the same will happen again, that new jobs will be created doing things which computers cannot do, like caring for people. Industries which do not even exist – in leisure and information, for example – will employ huge numbers.

But does history always repeat itself? Can we rely on things 'sorting themselves out'?

Why should people want to change jobs from an old industry to a new one if it also means moving house, changing schools, and parting with friends?

7 x 40 hours = 280 hours   1 in 7 unemployed

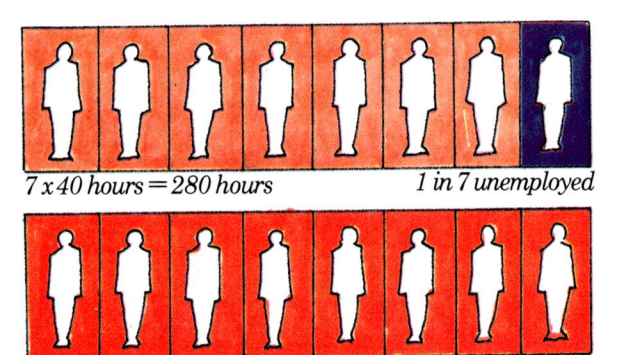

8 x 35 hours = 280 hours   Zero unemployed

Above *How a small reduction in average working hours would eliminate unemployment.*
Below *While some people are unemployed, others have more work than they can cope with.*

One of the annoying things about unemployment is that there are some people who are doing more work than they want to, at the same time as others are out of work. The obvious answer is to share work more equally, so that everybody can work and nobody has to work too much.

This can be done in many ways. The first is to cut working hours. Already, over the last hundred years, the average working week has dropped from about eighty to forty hours a week. Some people already work thirty-five hours or even less. A cut in the average hours from forty to thirty-five would provide nearly one extra job in seven – practically eliminating unemployment.

Workers could take longer holidays. They could take long periods off work, allowing them to study, to pursue hobbies or to travel.

People could retire earlier, so that they could have time to do some of the things that they had promised themselves when they were younger.

People could spend more time in education. You might, for example, leave school quite young, but go back to college from time to time during your life – a few months here, a couple of years there – to study new subjects that interest you, or which you think would be useful in your work.

But there are problems with all these suggestions. People who have work usually need, or think they need, all the money that they earn. They are not willingly going to accept shorter hours or longer holidays if it means earning less pay.

How many people with families to support are going to be able to return to college if this means losing income, which it usually does today?

Firms or even nations cannot just

decide to pay the extra cost. Competition dictates that they must reduce costs as far as possible.

For example, if a printing company introduces computers to set up the pages of type (computerized typesetting), it will need fewer workers – it cannot just pay its existing work force the same amount for doing less work. If it does, a rival firm in another town will be able to charge less for its printing. The first company then risks going out of business, and with the likely consequence of having to dismiss *all* its workers.

Even early retirement causes problems. Many elderly people prefer working: when they retire they may get bored and lose their sense of purpose, just like younger unemployed people.

Above *In the age of computers, we will study and explore new subjects to do with leisure.*

Below *The new and traditional methods of typesetting.*

Working life

We work for two reasons. The first reason is to feed and clothe ourselves and those who depend on us. The second reason is to give ourselves a sense of purpose in life, to help keep ourselves happy.

We now rarely need to work in order to stay alive – society will usually make sure we do not starve. But people still need to work in order to get a standard of living higher than the minimum level which the state provides.

Even if people are prepared to live cheaply, they still usually feel the need to work. Sociologists – people who study society – use the word 'alienation' for the feeling that people get if they do not believe they are doing something useful or fulfilling with their lives.

Some people believe that we must now change our traditional belief that work is important to us. The 'Protestant work ethic', as it is called, which developed with the Protestant religions before and during the Industrial Revolution, stresses the value of hard work. But now this ethic, this belief, is out of date, for it is unlikely that there will be enough jobs to go round.

In this case we need to re-educate people in their attitudes to work and leisure: to make them realise that they are not worthless just because they are unemployed, and to educate them into using their leisure time in ways which they find rewarding and which are

Below *Unemployment can be seen as a time of boredom and unhappiness* or *as an opportunity to find rewarding things to do.*

useful to society as a whole. But it is not easy to change the beliefs with which we have been brought up.

For those who will be working, computers will change the pattern of their working lives. Because computers can easily communicate along telephone lines, many office workers will no longer need to work in an office – they can just as easily have their computer terminal at home, and talk to people over the telephone when they need to.

Their firms will not need to rent so much expensive office space in city centres, and the workers will not have to spend as much money and time on commuting to work.

But this will bring other changes and cause other problems. People who need daily human contact will find that working at home makes them feel isolated. Many housewives have suffered from depression as a result of being alone at home all day.

Many people will not want to work at

Below *Computers will enable many office workers to work from home, but this may bring problems in the form of feelings of isolation and the desire for more human contact.*

Below *Local offices enable people who work for different organizations to share the same building and facilities.*
Bottom *Unskilled work will not change much in the age of computers.*

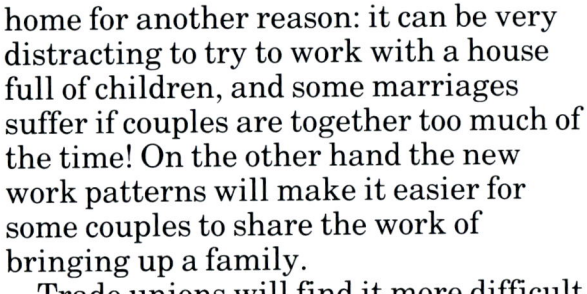

home for another reason: it can be very distracting to try to work with a house full of children, and some marriages suffer if couples are together too much of the time! On the other hand the new work patterns will make it easier for some couples to share the work of bringing up a family.

Trade unions will find it more difficult to organize, with their members spending most of their time at home.

Local offices may be the answer to the problems of working at home. People working for several different firms will come together to work at a building close to where they live, so that they can share facilities and meet other people.

Many of those who have work will be working with computers, and computers have been criticized for de-skilling work. 'De-skilling' means taking the skill out of work so that, for example, the person operating a computerized machine may be just a machine minder, doing what the machine says. There may be no opportunity to think, or to contribute personally to the way that the work is done.

How rewarding is it to work with computers themselves? It is hard to tell how much computers will affect our levels of satisfaction at work. It is important that people who design computer systems make sure that the people who use them still find their work satisfying.

Computers take away semi-skilled work – routine work which needs little thought. Unskilled work – street sweeping and other manual tasks – will not change much. Many other jobs will need *more* skill than before. This is because people will need to know how to use the computer as well as how to do the job they have done before. The more sophisticated a computer system is, the more training you need to make good use of it.

Below *Computers will make skilled work, such as tool making and design, even more skilful.*
Bottom *Robots will replace humans in routine, semi-skilled work.*

Working with computers

Because computers threaten to make so many changes to our working lives, it is natural that a critical eye has been turned on the computer itself. Does working with a computer harm you?

A lot of research has been done into the hazards of working with computers, and so we can hope that computers will be well designed.

It is important that you can sit comfortably when using a computer terminal, and see the screen clearly without having to strain your eyes, particularly if you are working with it for a long time.

Ergonomists – people who study the way machines can be used conveniently by people – have worked out the things that you need to be careful of in order to avoid eyestrain, aching backs or muscular problems. These ailments can all be caused by a badly planned work arrangement.

The keyboard itself should be at the right height – as close as possible to your knees – so that you can key without having to tense your body. The screen should be where you can see it clearly without suffering from distracting reflections from overhead lighting. The lettering on the screen should be very clear to read.

Are the ergonomics of any computers that you use as good as this? If not, get them corrected before you get backache

Above *The introduction of computers will not always lead to improved working conditions.*

and eye strain.

There is no evidence that a well-designed computer installation does any harm to its users. But we can never prove that it is completely safe. It could be, for instance, that the slight radiations from the video screen are harmful over a very long period, although most experts believe that they are harmless.

It is not only the computer hardware – the machine itself – which must be properly designed. The software – its programs – must also be well thought out so that the computer is easy to use.

It is not right to assume that somebody who is using a computer is an expert, or that the person should be prepared to spend a lot of time getting to learn the program. Programs should be made fool-proof and easy to use.

They should be written in such a way that the user is always told – or able to find out without having to look it up in a manual – what courses of action are open: the program itself should teach the user how to make it work.

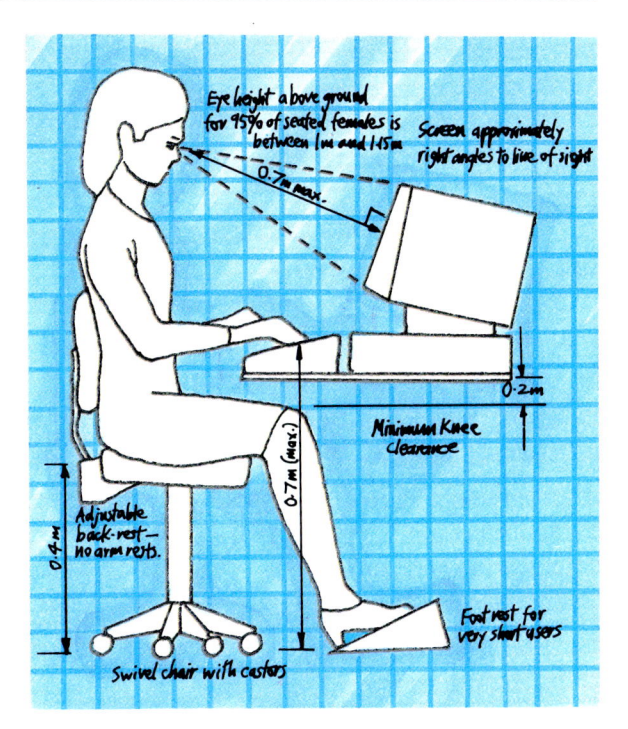

Above *A computer terminal should be well-designed.*
Below *A well-planned office.*

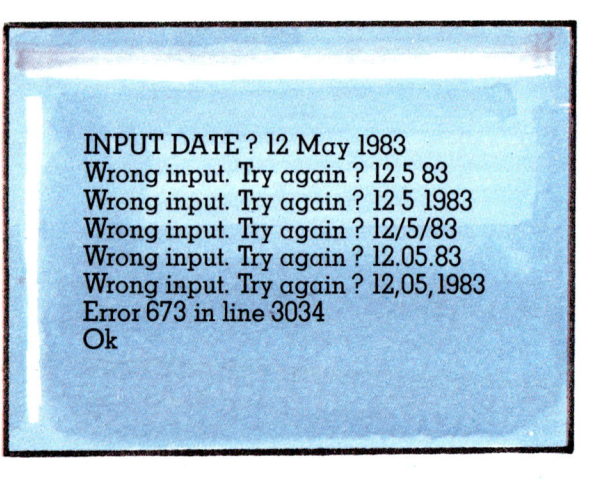

```
INPUT DATE ? 12 May 1983
Wrong input. Try again ? 12 5 83
Wrong input. Try again ? 12 5 1983
Wrong input. Try again ? 12/5/83
Wrong input. Try again ? 12.05.83
Wrong input. Try again ? 12,05,1983
Error 673 in line 3034
Ok
```

```
1.  Directory – list of files and sizes
2.  Copy a file
3.  Erase a file
4.  Edit a file – view it and change it
5.  Change a file's name
0.  Main menu
?   Help! – more information
    about files
```

The commands that you have to give the computer should be easy to use and easy to remember. You will probably not be using the program every day, and you do not want to have to learn it over again each time you do.

It is inevitable that you are going to make errors, whether it is because you do not understand what you are supposed to be doing, or just because you hit the wrong key. A program should allow you to make mistakes without making the computer 'crash'. A crash is when the computer stops doing what you want it to do, and loses the work you have done.

Whenever you are testing a program make sure that you give it a lot of *wrong* answers and that it reacts to them properly!

Left *An unfriendly screen display (top) and a helpful computer menu.*

Make sure, too, that the computer system is helpful when something goes wrong. A computer which just says 'ERROR' or 'ERROR 237' is not helpful. It should tell you, in your own language, what is wrong and what you should do. Unfortunately, many computers, particularly the cheaper ones, do not do this. So you need to know a fair amount about the system before you can get out of trouble.

Whatever the faults of computers, it is still true that they can be a lot of fun. Many people really enjoy using them. So much so that this can cause another problem – computerholism.

If 'alcoholism' means being addicted to alcohol, so that you cannot live without alcohol, then 'computerholism' is being addicted to computers.

This may quite easily happen when you get involved in a computer game or in a programming problem which is so challenging that you cannot leave it. You keep on at the computer long after you should have stopped to do some work or gone to bed.

Normally this does not matter. But some people allow the computer to take over their lives completely, so that they spend all their time with the computer and lose all contact with people. It can happen at school, at home or at work. Is that healthy?

Below *People can become addicted to computers at home or at work.*

Education and training

It is clear that education and training are going to be even more important in the computer age than they are today. Education is a way of reducing unemployment, and of making sure that people have skills which are needed.

Below *Adults as well as children will be using computers to learn new skills.*

In a world which is changing as rapidly as ours, it is going to be important to prepare ourselves to learn new skills. The skills which people learn when they first start work are likely to be out of date within a few years.

Your job will be much more rewarding if you are doing work which is actually needed. That means work which cannot be done better or faster by machine, work which uses your human skills. But that means you must have up-to-date skills. The best way to keep up to date is to go back to school or college from time to time, to learn a new subject or skill, or to refresh your knowledge of an old one.

Computers will not only drive many of us back to education, they will also be doing the teaching in schools and colleges.

Computers can be a very good aid for education. They can present information in a logical way, and test at each stage that it has been learnt. They give you encouragement for what you have learnt, so making you keen to carry on. They can set targets to challenge you and keep your interest.

They allow you to learn at your own speed, so that the faster student need not be bored and the slower one does not get muddled and left behind. They can even allow you to follow up your own interests in a way which is impossible to do in a large class.

At the moment, computers are still

Above *At the moment, computers are not very good at teaching us creative or social skills.*

quite expensive so that few schools can afford to have enough computers to allow everybody as much time on the computer as they might want.

Computer learning can be overdone. Computers cannot teach us everything that we need to know in life – how to relate to other people and how to work cooperatively, for instance. Nor are they very good at the moment at teaching us how to think creatively. They are excellent at teaching facts and techniques. But that is only a part of what learning is about.

Big Brother

One of the major criticisms that have been voiced about computers is that they make it too easy to invade our privacy. It is too easy to use the power of the computer to find personal and damaging information about individuals.

In George Orwell's book *1984* written in 1949, the totalitarian, non-democratic government of 1984 is able to keep an eye on all its citizens, thanks to television cameras in every room and a large intelligence service devoted to gathering information. Any form of free speech or objection to the government is therefore impossible. Its slogan is 'Big Brother is watching you'.

George Orwell has been shown to be a

Left *In Orwell's book, 1984, the government kept an eye on all its citizens with the aid of television cameras in every room.*
Below *The police can use computer-controlled television cameras to assist them with crowd control.*

pessimist: his idea of society has not yet arrived, although many elements of it are real enough, both in the 'free world' and in dictatorships.

George Orwell did not foresee the use of computers, for they would have made Big Brother's watching very much easier. Computers can be used by the state, companies or individuals to invade the privacy of the person in the street.

Why does privacy matter? If we don't do anything wrong, why should it matter what people know about us?

It matters for two reasons. Firstly, we cannot trust other people to deal with information about us in the way that *we* would like. They may have different views about how important something is. They may have different moral views.

For example, perhaps you once stole some money at school. You do not think that it is important any more and it was long ago. One day you are applying for a job, but the employer finds out about your theft and decides not to risk giving you a job. Would you feel that this is fair?

Secondly, the information may be wrong. Perhaps it was not you that stole the money at all, but somebody with a similar name. *You* do not even know that the employer knows about the theft, and you are not told the real reason why you have been turned down for the job. So you are not even given the opportunity to deny the allegation.

People do not need computers to invade your privacy – as George Orwell showed. But computers make snooping very much easier and more efficient.

Above *Television cameras linked to computers can be used to invade people's privacy.*

Below *Using central computer files, police forces are fast replacing old-fashioned methods of information gathering and retrieval.*

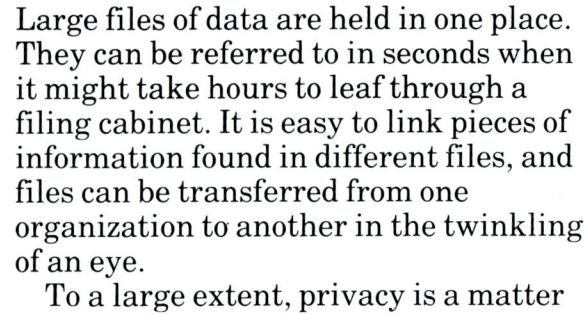

Large files of data are held in one place. They can be referred to in seconds when it might take hours to leaf through a filing cabinet. It is easy to link pieces of information found in different files, and files can be transferred from one organization to another in the twinkling of an eye.

To a large extent, privacy is a matter of making sure that information stays in the right place. You are happy for your doctor to have records about your health, but you may not want that information to get into the hands of your employer.

A number of policies have been suggested to reduce the risk that private information will be abused. Here are some of the policies:

1. People should be told that information about them is on file.
2. They should have the right to see the contents of files about them, and correct them if they are inaccurate.

3. Information should not be used for a different purpose than the one for which it was collected, except with the permission of the person concerned.
4. Information should be made secure so that people who are not entitled to it cannot get hold of it.

But even if these rules were put into effect, there would always be possibilities for abuse, by people who disobey the rules.

Should the rules extend to government security services? Some people think that government services which are protecting the state against subversion and terrorism should be exempt from such laws. But can you always trust all of those who work for the government agencies? Will *they* always get the right information and use it properly?

Invasions of privacy can be for the public good. In the hunt for a mass murderer, it may be useful to put on a computer file every little bit of gossip which may not be relevant or even true. The computer may be able to draw together apparently unimportant facts to point to a suspect.

The result may be that a vicious murderer is arrested before killing again. But what is the cost in terms of inaccurate and malicious information which could damage a lot of other people?

How can people be protected as far as possible from crime at the same time as having their privacy protected?

Medical records should obviously be kept confidential. But if records are put together centrally and processed by a computer, it can show trends in diseases so that their cause can be discovered and lives saved. How can this be done, whilst protecting the patients' privacy?

Below *If rumours are put on to a computer file, they could be used to track down criminals.*

Computers and the developing world

The world's rich, developed countries have often been criticized for trading with the poorer, developing countries with no heed to what is best for the latter. Are they using computers in the same way?

Top *Powerful microscopes are used in the assembly of computer chips.*

Above *In developing countries, the young women who retire from chip-assembly work because of deteriorating eyesight may find it difficult to re-adjust to a more traditional life.*

Computer chips themselves are often assembled in developing countries. Malaysia, Singapore, Hong Kong and other countries in the Far East all have chip-assembly plants.

The chips are made in highly automated plants in countries like the USA and Japan, and are then flown to less developed countries to be sealed in their plastic packages. The work entails soldering very fine wires between the chip and the metal legs of the outer package – the part we actually see.

The work involves looking through a microscope which rapidly produces eyestrain. Conditions in the factories are very good compared with most other factories in the developing world. However, because it is such fine work the young women who do it have to retire at an early age – in their thirties – when they can no longer see well enough to do it properly.

It is women who do the work because they have the small fingers and dexterity needed for such fine work. But women do not usually go out to work in these countries, and so the computer age is causing radical changes to the way their societies live.

The work the women do is well paid by their standards, although wages are only one twentieth of what they would be in rich countries. When they retire, the women then face new problems of adjusting back again to a more traditional life – they probably will not be able to find such well-paid work again.

Some people in developed countries complain that the work is being done in other countries when there is high unemployment at home. They call for customs' duties to be levied on the imports of chips, to encourage the manufacturers to get them assembled at home.

Others say that developing countries need the work more and should be encouraged to open more factories. But it is clear that these developments – like practically all social or economic changes – are not painless.

Left *Many people in Western countries protest that the new factories being opened in developing countries contribute to high unemployment at home.*

Technology should be 'appropriate'. That is to say, it should suit the circumstances of the people who will be using it: it should cost a price that they can afford; it should fulfil a real need; it should use local skills and resources; and it should fit in with the local social framework.

How appropriate are computers to the developing world?

Large computers are rarely appropriate in developing countries: they are expensive to buy; difficult to run – they need air conditioning and more reliable electricity supplies than are available; and they are expensive to look after – parts are difficult to obtain and there are few skilled engineers to maintain them.

As computers get smaller, more reliable, and easier to use, they become more appropriate to the needs of developing countries. However, before

Left and below *There is an enormous difference between the traditional technologies of developing countries and computer technology.*

they can be widely used, the price must drop drastically – even a small transistor radio may represent several years' saving for somebody living off the land.

Once in use, computers will start to bring useful skills into villages where skills have been scarce. Semi-skilled medical orderlies will be able to use them to help diagnose illnesses and suggest remedies, despite the lack of doctors.

Teachers who have never had a good enough training themselves will be able to use computers in their schools to provide expert knowledge expertly taught.

With modern telecommunications linking the remotest villages via satellite radio stations to the developed world, much of the world's knowledge will be available to everybody. This will help to overcome the information gap, which is bigger and even harder to bridge than the gaps of income, health and nourishment dividing the rich world from the poor.

Computers will be used in different ways to those which are common in developed countries. They will not be for personal use, but will be attached to schools and community centres – used for serious purposes like study and getting information, rather than for playing games.

They will be more appropriate and more useful than the computer giants of today, whose role in developing countries is often only to bring prestige to the people that buy them.

Above *Education and health care are just two of the good uses which computers can be put to in developing countries.*

War and peace

The history of computers has been closely bound up with man's search for better ways of fighting and destroying in war. Today they form an essential part of many weapons.

The first computers were used for decoding enemy communications during the last war, for calculating the trajectories of shells and missiles, and for designing the atomic bomb.

Since then many of the developments in computers – particularly in making them smaller – have been first made for military purposes before later being released to the civilian world. The huge amounts of money which are spent for

Top *An early-warning radar station (right), and the control centre of an air defence system.*
Left Colossus, *the British codebreaking computer (1943).*

Top to bottom *Computers form a vital part of the navigation, defence, and weapon-directing systems of land, air and sea forces.*

research and development in defence have accelerated the birth of the microcomputer by many years.

Computers are used in monitoring systems. These are designed to give early warning of an enemy attack, and it is ironical that here computers may be at their most dangerous. There have been many false alarms when computer errors have caused emergency alerts as if an enemy attack was taking place. There have been so many false alarms that it is now doubtful that anybody would believe them should one of the alerts turn out to be real!

Computers are also a vital part of systems for attack. Aircraft, tanks and ships rely heavily on many microcomputers for navigation, finding the enemy, communicating with friendly forces, and for directing weapons at enemy targets.

Some of the most deadly weapons are completely computer controlled. There are missiles which can be launched from ships, land or from aircraft far away from their moving target. They find the target by radar, or by using heat-seeking sensors. Then the computer corrects the missile's course as often as needed to keep it locked on to its target.

Other missiles are aimed at stationary targets on land. Their computers are programmed with the exact location of the target. Then the missile is launched and flies close to the ground, following the contours of the

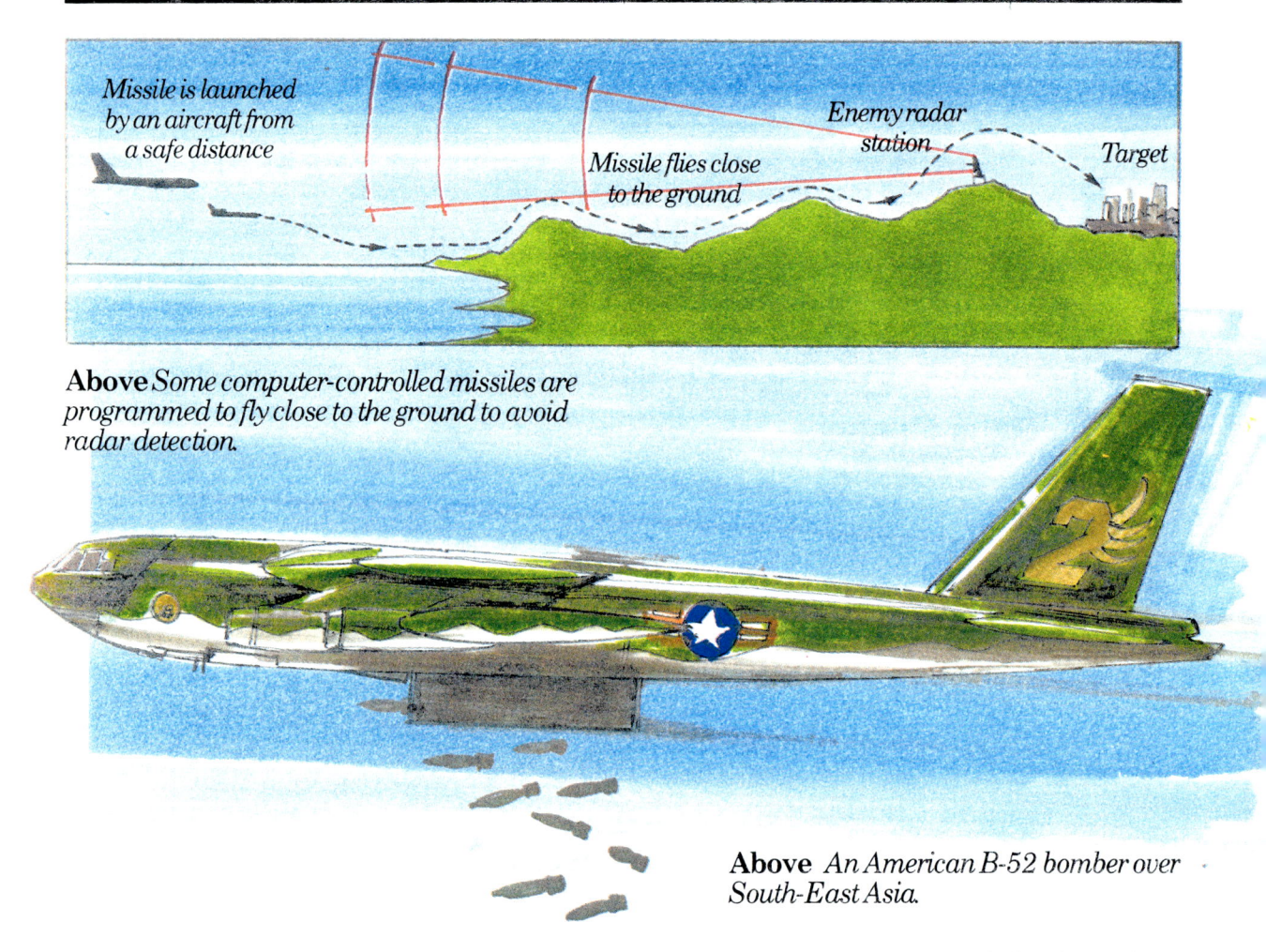

Above *Some computer-controlled missiles are programmed to fly close to the ground to avoid radar detection.*

Above *An American B-52 bomber over South-East Asia.*

land, too low to be picked up by the enemy radar. Its computer controls the distance from the ground and navigates it accurately to its target, perhaps many thousands of miles away.

It has been suggested that the super-intelligent computers of the future may refuse to obey commands to start a war because they will 'know' that it would be impossible to win such a war. But such hopes are surely wishful thinking.

Computers are always too vulnerable to the people who program them. Whether by design or by mistake, they are more likely to cause a military disaster than to preserve the world from it.

During the Vietnam War, computers were deliberately programmed to mislead American generals back in the USA about the targets which were being bombed. The US Air Force did not have government consent to bomb Cambodia, but Cambodia was being bombed. In the reports which were sent back to the USA, targets in Cambodia were automatically changed on the computer tapes so that they appeared to be targets in Vietnam.

The use of computers in weapons of war or in warning systems is no comfort to us. They may mean that somebody has more reliable information about attacks. But there is no guarantee at all that the people who receive that information will interpret it correctly, or make a sensible response.

Will computers need us?

As computers get more and more advanced, they will be able to do more and more of the work that the human brain does today. Will they eventually become cleverer than we are?

It is only forty years since the first electronic computers were built. During that short period, developments have been unbelievably fast: computers have become very powerful and very compact. Computer software has developed almost as fast: programs running on the smallest computers can now solve problems and provide information which would have been beyond human powers only thirty years ago.

Yet in many ways computers are still very stupid compared with human beings. They can only remember a small fraction of the information which even a young child knows. They are poor at recognizing shapes and interpreting what they see; at balancing, moving and using tools; and at creating new ideas. As a device for interpreting and

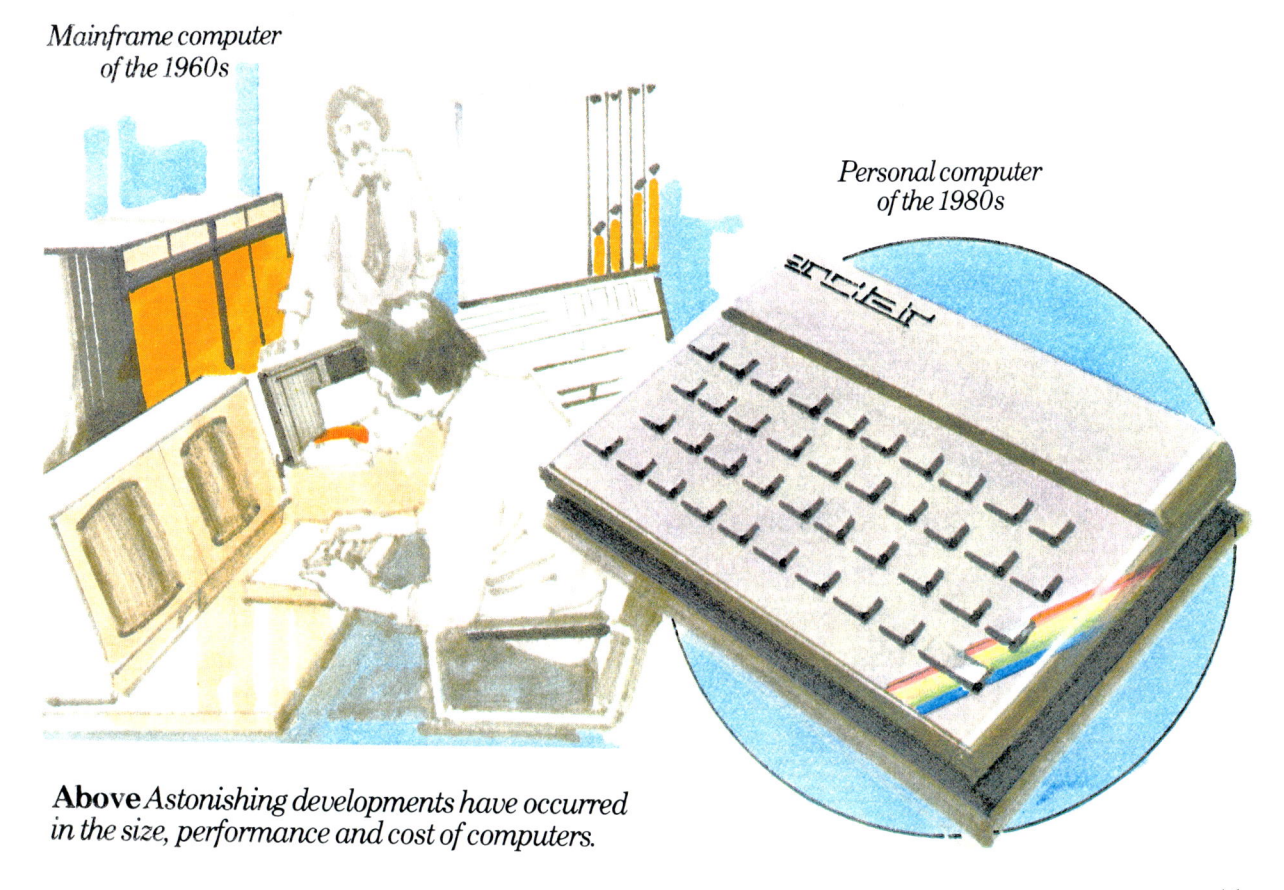

Mainframe computer of the 1960s

Personal computer of the 1980s

Above *Astonishing developments have occurred in the size, performance and cost of computers.*

remembering information, the human brain packs into a few cubic centimetres vastly more power than the biggest computer uses.

Few computer experts are prepared to say that computers will always be so stupid compared with people. Some peope try to argue that computers can never be 'intelligent' in the way that humans are. But however you try to define intelligence, you can quickly find examples of computers showing 'intelligence'. It is impossible to draw a firm line between the things that a computer can do and the things that a human brain can do, unless you use ideas like the 'soul' which cannot be proven scientifically.

One argument is that computers can never be truly 'intelligent' because they must always be programmed – they can only deal with information that they have been given. They can never 'create' like a human can. But humans, too, are programmed, for they can only deal with information that they have been given. Creativity and invention result from putting together established ideas in new ways and recognizing the combinations which work best.

Computers are very good at putting together different pieces of information: provided they have enough memory, they can compare and associate different items at a speed many times faster than a person. For this process to be useful the computer must be able to recognize which associations are useful. This means that it must be programmed, so that it 'knows' what the goals are, what a 'good' result is. Using such processes, computers can already defeat at chess all but the most brilliant human chess players. And there is no reason why, eventually, they should not be programmed to write 'good' poetry.

Above *How the programmer is 'programmed' by information from many different sources.*

Whilst computers are still a long way from reaching this goal, the gap may close in only a few decades. Computers do not have to imitate all the powers of the human brain. We can select only those activities which are useful to us, and concentrate on developing them. A computer for playing chess does not need to be able to smell, walk, swim, or write. So it is comparatively easy to develop a computer which can play chess as well as a human can.

There is no good reason why computers should not eventually be able to do the work of a doctor or a judge. They will also be able to invent things and even to build computers. How far will this go? Will computers need us? Or will they ultimately be able to do everything that we can do – except enjoy themselves? And if we get to that stage, then what sort of a life will it be for humans?

Above and left *Computers can be useful, creative tools for artists, musicians and poets.*
Below *These two computers are playing each other at a game of chess. How much further will computers develop and be able to do everything that we can do?*

Glossary

Allegation An unproved statement or assertion.
Automated Running automatically, without human intervention.

Blacklist A list of people who are considered untrustworthy.

Carbon dioxide A gas which is common in the air.
Cataract A disease which turns the lens of the eye cloudy, causing partial or complete blindness.
Chip A small sliver of silicon which can contain many thousands of electronic circuits.
Commute To travel to work from the suburbs to the centre of a city or town.
Computer A machine which gets information, changes and organizes it, stores it, and puts in out in a new form when needed.
Confidential Spoken, written or given in secret or private.

Dexterity Skill or nimbleness of the hands.
Dictatorship A country governed by a ruler or rulers with absolute power.

Dissident A person who disagrees with the government.

Ecology The study of plants and animals in relation to the environment.
Energy intensive Using energy in large amounts.
Erosion The eating away or wearing away of the land by the weather.

Microcomputer A computer based on a microprocessor. While a microcomputer usually means a complete microcomputer system with input, output and storage, the word is sometimes used for the actual microprocessor chip.

Microelectronics The use of electrical devices in which many components are formed together into small circuits on the surface of single chips.

Microprocessor A term which is normally used to mean the single chip containing the unit in which processing of data takes place, but it can also be used to mean the complete microcomputer system.

Oxygen A gas which humans need to breathe in order to live.

Pessimist A person who expects the worst or sees the worst in all things.

Program Instructions which are written into a computer to make it work.

Recession A temporary depression in economic activity or prosperity.

Scanner A device which uses a beam to scan an object or scene and transforms the reflected beam into digital patterns.

Sensor A device which senses something that is happening – for reading fluctuating temperatures or recording movement, for example.

Software The programs which a computer uses.

Solder A mixture of tin and lead which, when heated to melting point, can be used to join some metals.

Subversion The act of bringing about the complete downfall or ruin of a government.

Telecommunications The science of communication over a distance, by telegraph, radio, telephone and television.

Terminal A device separate from a computer for keying in information and displaying it.

Terrorists People who use violence and intimidation to achieve some goal.

Totalitarian Belonging to a one-party state which regulates every realm of life.

Trajectory The path taken by an object as it travels through the air.

Transistor An electronic component which can be used as a switch.

Vacuum tube The American word for an electronic valve.

Valve An electronic valve or thermionic valve is a vacuum-filled glass tube which can be used as an amplifier or a switch.

Word processing An office procedure for storing, editing and manipulating text using an electronic keyboard, computer and printer.

Finding out more

Books

You may want to start finding out more about computers by reading the other books in this series:

Computers in Everyday Life tells how we will be using computers in our daily lives.

How Computers Work explains what the different parts of a computer do and how they are made.

The Story of Computers tells of their history and development.

Robots and Intelligent Machines is about computers at work and on the move.

Programming Computers talks about the languages we use to get computers to work for us.

If you browse in your local book store or library you will find a number of other books on computers. Titles to look for on the social implications of computers include Christopher Evans's books, *The Mighty Micro* (Gollancz, 1979) and *The Making of the Micro* (Gollancz, 1981); and *The Microchip: Appropriate or Inappropriate Technology* by Alan Burns (John Wiley, 1981).

Books about computers in general include *The Silicon Chip* by Dr Ken Woodcock (Wayland, 1980); *The Computer Age* by Martin Campbell-Kelly (Wayland, 1978); *Scelbi's Secret Guide to Computers* by Russell Walter (Scelbi, 1981); Peter Large's *The Micro Revolution* (Fontana, 1979), and Adam Osborne's *Running Wild: the next industrial revolution* (Osborne/McGraw-Hill, 1979).

Magazines

There are a number of general magazines about microcomputers, which sometimes write about the way computers are affecting our lives. British magazines include *Personal Computer World* and *Practical Computing*. *Computing Today* specializes in the computer hobbyist. *Microcomputer Printout* is also good. American magazines include *Byte*, *Interface Age* and *Microcomputing*.

New Scientist is a general magazine which often discusses the social impact of technology. *New Society* and *Undercurrents* deal with social and ecological issues, including technology. *The New Internationalist* writes about the problems of the developing countries.

Computers

You can also use computers to find out about computers. In the UK, *Prestel* carries computer programs and information about clubs (which you can also get from some of the computer magazines).

Computerized Bulletin Boards are also spreading in several countries. Your computer talks to another computer over the telephone and you can look at messages and fetch games and programs on to your own computer. You may be able to do this from your school, although somebody will have to pay for the telephone call!

Index

Artificial limbs 6

Central heating 7, 14
Changing jobs 17
Communication 6
Computerholism 27
Computers
   ailments associated with 8, 24-5
   and chess 43
   components of 12, 13
   'crash' 26
   design of 24, 25
   diminishing size of 13, 41
   and environment *see* Ecology
   and information 6, 7, 11, 17, 30-33
   intelligence of 41-3
   medical applications 6-7
   in schools and colleges 28-9
   and war *see* War and peace
   and work arrangement 24-5
   writing poetry 42
'Computopia' 6-7
'Computyrannia' 8-9
Crime prevention 7, 8-9
Customs duties 35

Design by computers 14-15

Ecology 7, 11, 12-15
Education and training 6, 11, 18, 23, 28-9, 37

Farming 15

Industrial Revolution 10, 17, 20

Leisure 6, 11, 17, 18, 20
Listing paper 14

Making payments 9
Microelectronic revolution 10

Natural resources 7, 12-13, 14

Oppression by the state 8-9, 30
Orwell, George 30, 31

Paperless office 14
Pollution 7
   see also Ecology
Privacy, invasion of 11, 30-33
Programs 14, 25-7, 41, 42
Progress and disruption 9, 10-11, 17
Protestant work ethic 20-21

Records
   government 33
   medical 7, 32, 33
Retirement 18, 19

Silicon chips 12, 35
Software *see* Programs

Terrorism 8, 33
Third World countries 7, 9, 11, 34-7
   appropriateness of computers to 35-7
   chip assembly plants 35
   and information gap 37
Trade unions 22
Transport 9

Unemployment 8, 16-19, 20

Vacuum tubes (valves) 13
Vietnam war 40

Index

War and peace 11, 38-40
    and birth of microcomputer 38-9
    warning systems 39, 40
    weapons 38-40
Waste, prevention of 15
Weather forecasting 15
Work 6, 8, 9, 11, 16-19, 20-23
    conditions of 6, 8, 9
    cut in working hours 18
    de-skilling 22-3
    done by robots 6, 8, 17
    from home 6, 21-22
    and job satisfaction 23
    and local offices 22
    semi-skilled 23
    sharing of 18